BEGINNING ARCHERY

ROY K. NIEMEYER
Michigan State University

WADSWORTH PUBLISHING COMPANY, INC.
Belmont, California

L.C. Cat. Card No.: 61-15840

Printed in the United States of America

Ninth printing: September 1966

CONTENTS

1

VALUES

The twang of a bowstring, the flight of an arrow speeding toward the gold, and the thud of an arrow hitting the target are thrills to the vast number of people who are archers. Archers by the thousands remain fascinated by the crude equipment that once served man as his chief weapon and means of survival. For modern man to have to depend on the bow and arrow for survival is almost unthinkable; however, archery has found its place as a sport in the life of modern man. What is it about this sport that keeps people participating and constantly attracts large numbers of newly interested people of all ages and both sexes?

It is difficult to point out any single reason for the popularity of archery. One of the physiological values derived through participation is the development of strength and endurance, especially in the musculature of the upper body. The contraction of the abdominal and back muscles with the expansion of the chest muscles aids in the development and maintenance of proper posture. A certain amount of eye exercise is obtained through the intense concentration on a focal point required for aiming. A substantial amount of all-round exercise is accrued through the walking and bending involved. It is for these reasons, and the fact that the sport is usually played in the healthful outdoors, that archery is a stimulating, invigorating pastime.

Social benefits for the archer include excellent opportunities to meet people of both sexes and all ages, to engage leisurely in the sport with a few friends on an informal basis, to compete extensively against others, to cooperate with other club members toward a common goal, to engage as a family in a recreational pursuit, or to understand human nature better through the opportunities provided while hunting and camping together.

There are other values in archery that are of a psychological nature. Real personal satisfaction can be derived through handling a bow competently. Fun, relaxation, and a sense of achievement at being able to place the arrow exactly where it is aimed are psychological

2

benefits that help build self-confidence. The opportunity to get away from it all, to pick up the bow and arrows and watch the arrows penetrate the target, may be just the thing to relieve pent-up emotions after a busy day. Another important psychological value is the pride of the bow hunter who bags his deer with a running shot at thirty yards, or who finally gets his deer after ten fruitless years.

Perhaps the finest long-range benefit of archery is the length of time that one is able to enjoy it. Shooting merely for recreation, engaging in tournaments from the local to the national or international level, having an activity that the whole family can enjoy together, and hunting and fishing with the bow are among the many activities archers enjoy. The latter activities often become the ultimate in archery for many people and whatever else is done in shooting is done as preparation for hunting or fishing.

Archery is classified as an individual activity, which means that no other person need be present for complete participation. Activities of this nature are necessary in the repertory of those who claim to be physically educated. One cannot participate in vigorous team activities for a lifetime. Sports such as football and basketball usually prove to be too strenuous and undesirable for most people after the age of thirty or thirty-five. It therefore behooves the athlete to learn some individual recreational activities. Athletes who reach the age of forty-five tend to become less active than nonathletes and consequently gain more harmful weight. Perhaps this is because the athletes can no longer engage in vigorous sports and have not learned worthwhile leisure-time sports. On the other hand, the nonathletes took time while they were young to learn carry-over sports, participated more, became proficient, and eventually controlled their weight better.

It is well known that people will play the games they play well. Consequently, it behooves one to learn some individual activities at the earliest age possible and to learn them well. "Be active for life" is sound advice from a health standpoint.

Among the most obvious advantages of archery over most other activities offered in the physical education program are that it can be enjoyed the year around, outdoors and indoors, is reasonably inexpensive, and can be enjoyed for life. Another distinct advantage is that a lifelong hobby may be realized in making tackle or collecting lore associated with archery.

HISTORY

The time and place of the origin of archery are not known, but drawings left by cavemen on the rock walls of their dwellings on the Spanish peninsula show that the bow and arrow was known at that time. Archaeologists estimate that archery was known about 100,000 years ago. It can safely be stated that the discovery of the bow and arrow was one of the most important cultural advances in the history of the human race. This discovery was just as important as, or perhaps more so than, the discovery of fire or the wheel, or the development of speech, for it was not until after the bow was developed that man became superior to the wild animals of his day, and this may have had a great influence on the very continuation of the human race.

The Discovery of the Bow

How archery was discovered may only be conjectured. Possibly a man idly experimenting with a tree branch and piece of vine, gut, or rawhide attached discovered that it could cast a light stick of wood farther than he could throw a heavier spear. The idea developed until better pieces of wood were found for bows and feathers or leaves were added to the sticks to guide them better in flight. The idea of adding sharp stones to the ends of the arrows was probably the next stage of development. Once the bow was perfected, it became man's most important weapon. We can imagine his feeling of relief when he no longer had to flee the beasts or to fight in close combat with clubs or spears.

Bow Known Widely

The bow is thought to have been known to all Eastern Hemisphere tribes except the aboriginal Australians. The Israelites, Babylonians, Mongolians, Assyrians, Chinese, and Japanese all favored the bow and arrow. The Egyptians used bows and arrows in overthrowing the Persians, their conquerors, and then successfully waged war on many other countries. The success of the bow and arrow as a weapon of war spread rapidly and many nations gave up their chief weapons—slings and javelins—for this more efficient device.

The Greeks and Turks are credited with originating composite bows made of wood, horn, and sinew and shaped like a "C" when unstrung. These composite bows were extremely efficient. Interestingly, many of our modern bows are tending to resemble them. An ancient Turkish bow is said to have shot an arrow over 800 yards. This record flight was unsurpassed until Danny LaMore won the National Flight Championship at Lancaster, Pennsylvania, on August 17, 1959, with a free-style flight (bow held by the feet and pulled with both hands) of 937.17 yards and a regular flight (hand-held) of 850.67 yards. At the same meet Norma Beaver set a women's national record with a 578.7-yard shot.

The bow remained the chief weapon of warfare for centuries until the battle of the Spanish Armada in 1588. For that battle, the English had experimentally equipped 10,000 of their troops with firearms with outstanding success. The bow soon became a secondary war weapon and after the last big battle was fought with bows and arrows by the Chinese at Taku in 1860, it became obsolete as a weapon of war. However, some primitive tribes in Africa and South America still employ bows and arrows in warfare (as is evidenced by small, slow-flying planes that become "pincushions" over certain jungle areas) and also depend on them as their chief means of taking game and fish.

Archery As a Sport

After the decline of the bow as a weapon, archery was forgotten until countries such as England saw its merit as a sport. King Henry VIII was an enthusiastic archer and an ardent bettor who staged large matches and invited wide participation. With the help of this kingly interest, archery became very popular in England, and proficiency in the use of the longbow was common.

Archery was known to the Indians of America when the Pilgrims arrived. The Indians soon gave up their bows and arrows for the more efficient firearms, and so history repeated itself. Archery began as an American sport in 1828 when a group of archers formed the United Bowmen of Philadelphia—still existing today. In 1879, the National Archery Association was founded and yearly tournaments began on the national level, the first being held in Chicago.

For over 100 years of American archery, target archery competition prevailed. In 1934, when the NAA held its tournament in Los Angeles, a group of archers mainly interested in bow hunting began agitating for a new kind of game that was suited for off-hand shooting, which was more usable for hunting. Six years later, in 1940, the National Field Archery Association was organized. For ten years competition was restricted to bare bow shooting or the use of a single pin sight. Today, field archery recognizes the values of the two main styles of shooting, and tournaments are conducted in two divisions, free style and instinctive.

The Future of Archery

The future of archery looks bright. Archery tackle sales are among the highest of all sporting goods and are still rising. People of all ages are taking up the sport. There were 1.7 million bow twangers in 1946, according to the National Recreation Association; in 1960 they numbered more than 4.7 million—up 176 per cent. The greatest increase can be seen in the large numbers of new licensed bow hunters each year. From 1950 to 1960, the number of licensed archery deer hunters in Michigan alone jumped from a few thousand to 40,000. Practically every state has special bow seasons which commonly precede the regular deer seasons, and usually last much longer. In Michigan, for example, the bow season is five weeks long, while the regular deer season is only fifteen days. Because archery has many merits, it is probable that people of all ages will continue to enjoy it in the years ahead.

Archery equipment is commonly called *tackle*. The only tackle absolutely necessary for participation is a bow with string attached and some arrows. However, if more comfort and efficiency are desired an arm guard and finger tab or glove must be worn at all times. To make tackle easier to carry, a quiver should be added to the tackle list.

BOWS

There are four main woods used in making self bows. A *self bow* is a bow made from one type of material, in contrast to the *laminated bow*, which is made of several pieces of wood or other materials glued together.

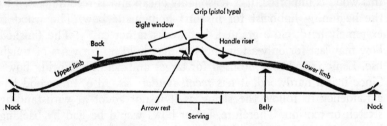

Illustration 1: A laminated bow

Probably the smoothest shooting self bow wood is yew. Yew is a type of cedar that grows in the Pacific Northwest. It is becoming rare, consequently expensive, and market conditions seem to indicate its coming obsolescence. Yet yew makes a wonderful longbow, especially for target archery, and will not soon be forgotten for its records have left their imprint for centuries. In making a yew bow some sapwood should be retained and used on the back of the bow for its elastic quality while the heartwood, better under compression, is used on the belly side.

7

A good hunting bow can be constructed from osage orange (*Bois d'Arc*), a hardwood tree sometimes called hedgewood, for it is often planted in rows to make hedges on farms ranging from Indiana to Texas. The tree is thorny and develops a warty, light green fruit the size of grapefruit, which is not edible. Selection of this wood for bow making presents problems as does the manufacture of it. The wood is extremely hard, sawing and planing are difficult, so scraping and sanding are much resorted to. The wood has been found to be better under *compression* than it is under tension. Consequently it is better used in the belly of the bow and backed with another wood such as hickory or with some other elastic material. However, good short bows can be made of osage orange and will withstand the abuse they are often subjected to under hunting conditions. It does not make an especially good target bow because it is rather *rough-in-hand* or tends to have kick or recoil qualities.

A third type of commonly used wood for making self bows is lemonwood. It is named after its creamy, lemon-like color rather than after the tree of which it is made. The tree is really *degame*, which grows around the Mediterranean and in Cuba. Even though this wood is imported, it is reasonably cheap and is recommended to the beginning hobbyist for his first homemade bow. The wood is extremely hard, close grained, but works rather easily. The finished bow may last for only a few shots or may hold up for years of rough use. Lemonwood may be used for target and field or hunting bows. Since it is a hardwood, it has *recoil tendencies*. Also, this wood has a tendency to follow the string as it is not adept at withstanding stretch or tension. Therefore, better bows would be had by backing lemonwood with a more elastic wood or other material.

Hickory is the fourth most commonly used self bow wood in the United States today. It is fairly abundant, but it is the least desirable of the four woods, because it does not stand compression, is slow in action, has much kick, has poor recovery, and follows the string badly. The best thing that can be said for hickory is that it has excellent stretch qualities; consequently, it can be used successfully to back other bow woods, especially osage orange.

Other self bows are made of solid Fiberglas, hollow Fiberglas, steel, and aluminum. The aluminum bows have lost a great deal of popularity because of the personal danger involved when the bows break. At the present time, Fiberglas bows are very popular, especially for beginners and children. They are durable, have good shooting qualities, stand up well under mistreatment; but they lack that smooth-in-hand quality that the more experienced archer seeks. The glass bows could ride a tidal wave in popularity if they were improved to the extent that the glass fishing rod was improved. Low cost and ease of production would favor the future use of Fiberglas bows.

The laminated recurved bow in all its beauty in color and design seems to be stealing the hearts of the more experienced archers. Coupled with gracefulness is a highly efficient, smooth shooting cast. A most interesting point about these modern bows is the similarity in material and design even though manufactured by different concerns. Most have maple cores and Fiberglas backs and bellies. Differences are noted mainly in the color and texture of the Fiberglas, the type and color of wood in the handle riser, the length of the bow, the amount of recurve, the weight, and whether the handle rises to the belly or to the back. Handle design is moving toward the pistol grip idea, which facilitates the use of the extended wrist.

Bows may vary in weight from 10 to 110 pounds. The ten-pounder might be ideal for the six-year-old, whereas an elephant hunter would use the heavier-weight bow. Bow weight is determined by the number of pounds of pull required to draw the string a specified distance. Most men's bows are measured at the 28-inch draw length. In Table 3-1 bow weights are suggested for men and women for different purposes.

TABLE 3-1
BOW WEIGHTS FOR MEN AND WOMEN

Use	Men	Women
Target archery	30–38 pounds	25–28 pounds
Field archery	35–42 pounds	25–32 pounds
Hunting * and fishing	42–52 pounds	30–45 pounds

* For certain bear, moose, lions, elephants, and other tough animals more weight may be necessary.

ARROWS

Arrows are the archer's most important equipment. (See Illustration 2 for arrow parts.) A good job of scoring can be done with an average bow and excellent arrows, but not with an excellent bow and low-quality arrows. Some qualities to seek in arrows include:

1. Matched spine—*spine* is the stiffness of the shaft as measured by a spinetester, which supports an arrow at two points 26 inches apart with a two-pound weight at the center of the shaft. See Illustration 3. If arrows having different spine tests are shot from the same bow they will have varying flights.

2. Matched for the bow—for each bow weight there is a proper spine test and this should be used for best results.

3. Matched weight—even though shafts may be the same thickness and length they may vary in weight because of the density of the wood. Using matched weight arrows is not generally required for beginning archers, but it becomes more important when better hits are desired.

4. Straight shafts—an arrow that is not straight has an erratic flight. Straightness is of extreme importance.

5. Identical length and thickness—it is dangerous to shoot arrows that are too short for the archer. Cast is lost if the arrows are too long, too thick, or too heavy.

6. Identical feathers—feathers should be evenly spaced and identical in height, length and shape of trim. Arrows may be straight or spiral fletched, right or left sided, or have three or four feathers, as long as each one in the set is identical with the others.

7. Nocks and piles should be securely held and placed straight.

8. Arrows should be well identified by an attractive crest.

Illustration 2: The arrow   *Illustration 3: A spinetester*

Wooden arrows are generally made of Port Orford cedar, Norway pine, or birch. Birch is least preferred because of its heavy weight and the fact that arrows made of it become crooked quite readily and are difficult to straighten. Very fine wooden arrows of compressed cedar are now available.

Arrows are also made of aluminum and Fiberglas. The expert or even the advanced archer should consider aluminum arrows because they are light and can be matched perfectly in spine and weight.

Fiberglas arrows are steadily being improved and are preferred by many good archers.

More important to the beginning archer than the arrow material is arrow length, for if an arrow is too short the archer may be seriously injured through the overdraw, and if it is too long, efficiency is lost. Three ways to check for proper arrow length are: (1) measure arm spread from fingertip to fingertip with arms extended sideways and refer to the arrow length chart in Table 3–2; (2) place a yardstick or long arrow against the breastbone (sternum) and extend both arms forward parallel to the floor and have a partner measure or mark the point to which the fingertips reach; and (3) attach a 30-inch shaft to the string of a light (15 to 20 pounds) bow (drill a hole through the shaft) and let the pile end run through a screw-eye at the arrow shelf; see Illustration 4.

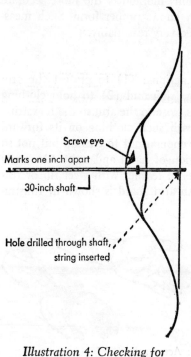

Screw eye

Marks one inch apart

30-inch shaft —

Hole drilled through shaft, string inserted

Illustration 4: Checking for proper arrow length

TABLE 3-2

ARROW LENGTH CHART

Arm Spread (inches)	Arrow Length (inches)
57–59	22–23
60–62	23–24
63–65	24–25
66–68	25–26
69–71	26–27
72–74	27–28
75–77	28–29
Over 77	30

The shaft should be marked at 1-inch intervals so the length of arrow drawn can be read as the archer draws the string and anchors at the appropriate anchor point. This method is the most accurate of those described if the supervisor knows proper form. Such measuring apparatus could be constructed very reasonably.

ARM GUARDS

An arm guard has two main functions: (1) to protect the arm from the slap or recoil of the bowstring and (2) to hold clothing such as long-sleeved shirts or jackets close to the arm so the bowstring will not be deflected by contact with such clothing on its forward progress. The guard should be stiff enough not to curl up but not so stiff that it will dig into the junction of hand and wrist. Generally the arm guards made of two pieces of leather with steel rib or ribs between prove most satisfactory. An arm guard is shown in Illustration 5.

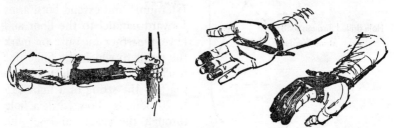

Illustration 5: Accessories

FINGER PROTECTION

Finger gloves or finger tabs are the commonly used finger protectors; see Illustration 5. Some sort of protection should be used for two reasons: (1) to protect the releasing fingers from the friction of the bowstring, and (2) to provide for a smoother release. The skin rolls toward the fingertips as the string passes over the unprotected, rolled-up flesh, resulting in a rough release; blisters may result from prolonged shooting unless the archer uses finger protection. Some experts have been eliminated in the midst of national tournaments because of blistered fingers, even though gloves were worn.

Finger gloves provide maximum protection because the three shooting fingers are completely surrounded with leather. Gloves are often clumsy to the beginner, but with practice, they become an asset. A stiffer leather, such as cordovan, is considered better than a soft cowhide.

A finger tab is a flat piece of leather that goes between the three shooting fingers and the string. Tabs are more reasonably priced than gloves, but they do not give maximum protection. Some users get blisters between the first and second fingers from the arrow nock. Certain experts, however, claim to get slightly more cast out of the bow by using a tab, and many target archers prefer tabs and claim to get a smoother release with them.

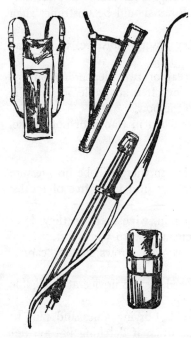

Illustration 6: Quivers

QUIVERS

Quivers have been designed for all purposes. Ground quivers, back quivers, and hip quivers are most commonly used in target archery. Ground quivers, which hold both bow and arrows, have proved to be very satisfactory for group instructional purposes.

Field archers generally use back, hip, and pocket quivers. The pocket quiver seems to be the most desirable.

Quivers used in hunting include: center back quivers, off-the-shoulder back quivers, hip quivers, arm quivers, and bow quivers. Because of the ease of maneuverability and arrow accessibility, the bow quiver is best for hunting most types of game. Various quivers are depicted in Illustration 6.

CARE, REPAIR, AND STORAGE OF EQUIPMENT

Inspect all equipment regularly; look especially for damaged arrows. An ounce of prevention is worth a pound of cure. Many little things that go wrong may be repaired before any injury or costly damage occurs.

Bows

1. Store bows in a cool, slightly humid place to retain flexibility. Hang them vertically on pegs by the string, or in clamps, or preferably lay them horizontally on two pegs. Bows should be unstrung when not in use.

2. Keep bows off the ground; they absorb moisture, which may cause warping or separating of laminations.

3. Refinish wooden bows every year or two, depending on the amount of use and condition of the bow. It is advisable occasionally to apply a good grade of floor wax to the bow.

4. Bow cases help to protect bows when in transit or not in use.

Arrows

1. Store arrows in a vertical position so there will be no pressure on the shafts to bend them. Keep arrows in a place free of moths; moths will eat the feathers.

2. If arrows get wet from grass or rain, wipe them so they don't absorb moisture. Wooden arrows generally warp when wet.

3. Destroy cracked or splintered wooden arrows so they cannot be used.

4. Nocks and points can be replaced by the novice at negligible cost.

5. Feathers may be replaced. Use fast-drying glues and pins to hold feathers in place while the glue dries, if fletching jigs are not available.

6. Arrows may be refletched completely or partially with a fletching jig.

7. Wooden arrows may be straightened by heating the warped area (preferably not over direct flame), rebending it, and allowing it to cool. Aluminum arrows may be straightened with an arrow tube straightener. An expert may be able to straighten an aluminum arrow by hand.

Bowstrings

1. Keep the bowstring well waxed. Use beeswax on all of the string except the center serving, which should be waxed with paraffin.
2. Replace frayed bowstrings before they break.

Accessories

1. Dry leather goods slowly if they are wet. Do not force drying by applying heat, since leather may crack and shrink.
2. Clean leather with saddle soap.

COST OF EQUIPMENT

Bows vary from $5.00 to $100.00 in cost. A bow for the beginning adult may be purchased for $20 to $30 and be completely satisfactory.

Arrows of wood range in cost from $2.50 to $18.00 a dozen. The beginning adult should get *matched* arrows at around $8.00 to $12.00 a dozen. Fiberglas and aluminum arrows are more costly.

Arm guards may be made from scrap leather or purchased at prices from $.75 to $3.50.

Finger protectors may be made from scrap leather or purchased at $.35 to $.75 for tabs, while gloves vary from $1.50 to $3.50.

4 TECHNIQUES OF PARTICIPATION

The bow must be strung before shooting. There are two acceptable ways of stringing the bow: the pull-push method and the step-in method. In Illustration 7 the pull-push method is shown. The bow is pulled by the handle while the upper limb is pushed down and the string slid up simultaneously. The bow is thus supported at three points and will bend evenly without undue stress at any point.

Illustration 7: Pull-push method   Illustration 8: Step-in method

In the step-in method, the right leg is put between the string and the belly of the bow (the belly faces forward). The lower end of the bow is placed above the instep of the left foot while the bow handle rests against the back of the thigh. The right hand is used to push the bow forward while the left hand guides the string into the nock. Avoid twisting the lower limb. See Illustration 8.

A person may be able to shoot a bow and arrow without being aware of the proper techniques, but he will not be able to shoot well unless he knows and uses them correctly. At first it is necessary to think about each fundamental movement as it is being performed, but when the fundamentals are learned they become habitually ingrained. It is important to begin correctly so that bad habits will not be developed.

THE TEN TECHNIQUES OF TARGET ARCHERY

The list of fundamentals could be combined under fewer topics, but in the final analysis ten important techniques of shooting should be mastered in order to shoot well. They are: stance, grip and bow arm, nocking, drawing, anchoring, relaxing, aiming, concentrating, releasing, and following through.

1. *Stance*—Stand with a feeling of stability, but avoid stiffness. The feet should be about shoulder width apart, straddling the shooting line with toes straight ahead. Weight should be evenly distributed, not concentrated on either foot or on the toes or heels only. The knees and legs should be relaxed and straight; the abdomen should be held in, not allowed to droop forward; the chest should be up and the entire body in good, erect posture with the body's weight resting on its bony structure. The stance should feel comfortable and relaxed. Stand at right angles to the target, the left side facing it, and the head turned toward the target.

2. *Grip and Bow Arm*—The grip and bow arm fundamentals are equal in importance, or more so, to the release, which is traditionally said to be the most important part of form. This can easily be seen when giving a little twist of the wrist to a bow with an arrow nocked. It takes only fractions of an inch of movement to make many inches of error on the target at twenty yards and beyond. Even a poor release can be partially overcome by having a steady bow arm and proper grip. However, poor bow arm fundamentals cannot be overcome by having a perfect release. Naturally, an archer would want to perfect both bow arm and release fundamentals.

The grip that seems to be best for most archers when the bow is not too heavy is the extended wrist grip as shown in Illustration 9. In this grip the bow handle is pushed with the "V" formed by the junction of the thumb and index finger while the wrist is raised and the fingers lowered. The bow is not gripped at all but rather is supported at maximum arm's length from the body. To keep the bow from falling from the hand at release, the index finger and/or the second finger are wrapped gently around the back of the handle. A slight pressure, which may help stabilize the bow, may be exerted on the sides of the handle by the thumb and index finger and the little finger may be lowered to touch the left edge of the bow below the handle or on the belly. The bones in the wrist should be straight, in alignment, and should "carry the load." Bending the wrist inward, outward, or downward puts musculature into action, which causes wrist movement on release. The bow arm should be fully extended but not locked stiff at the elbow. Rather, the elbow should be turned outward to avoid being

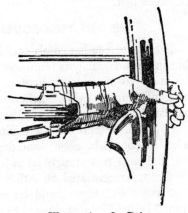

Illustration 9: Grip

hit by the bowstring. The shoulder must be kept down and back. The whole arm should simulate a right angle brace on a post (the body) and should be held just as steady (without tenseness, however).

3. *Nocking*—The act of putting the arrow on the string is called *nocking*. To do this, place the bow in a horizontal position so the back of the left hand is pointing up. Take the arrow by the nock, hold it between the thumb and index finger of the right hand, and slide it across the arrow rest (on the left side of the bow) and string with the cock feather up. When the nock end of the arrow reaches the string, remove the index finger from it and reach around and under the string and regrasp the nock. Pull the nock backwards, positioning it onto the string at the nocking point. The arrow may now be supported against the bow with the index finger of the bow hand

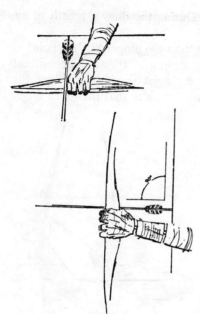

Illustration 10: Nocking

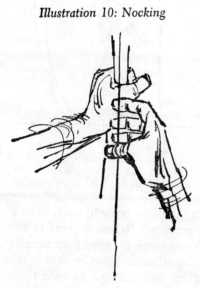

Illustration 11: Grasping the string

until the string is partially drawn, but this will not be necessary every time. The arrow should be nocked at a 90-degree angle with the string and top of the arrow rest. The nocking point should be marked with ink or a nock stop should be constructed on the string. See Illustration 10 for proper nocking technique.

4. *Drawing*—Drawing, pulling, or spreading the bow involves many of the upper body muscles, but in particular the upper arm, shoulder, and upper back muscles. Place the first three fingers of the right hand on the string, having the arrow nock between the first and second fingers. Position the fingers on the string so they grasp it as far to the ends as possible for comfort and safety. The string may be grasped at the first joint, not above, but it is better to have the string nearer the fingertips as this provides a smoother release (less movement involved). See Illustration 11.

The fingers should form a hook and should be relaxed during the draw. Tenseness in the hand must be eliminated; *avoid hooking the hand.* The act of drawing is a simultaneous action of both arms. The bow arm is raised toward the target while the string arm pulls backward. Back, shoulder, and upper arm muscles are chiefly used during this spreading of the arms. During the draw a breath of air should be taken and held.

5. *Anchoring*—Coming to a consistently proper anchor point is of extreme importance. Much variance results through inconsistent anchoring. The best anchor point for sight shooting is under the chin. The string hand should be pulled back so that the index finger comes under the tip of the chin and the string bisects the front of the chin. The head should be held forward enough so the tip of the nose is also bisected by the string. If the string is drawn to the chin and nose each time, a full draw results each time and thus consistency will develop. See Illustration 12.

That consistency must be achieved for best results cannot be overemphasized. Even an eighth of an inch of variance in anchoring will mean a significant error on the target.

6. *Relaxing*—At full draw, there should be a conscious effort made to relax. Any athlete will perform better if relaxed rather than tense. The archer at full draw should try to settle down on his bones. That is, body muscu-lature should not be supporting body weight, but the lines of

Illustration 12: The anchor point

force should go through the bone structure. Any muscles that are tense should be made to relax. Relaxa-tion can be learned and should be practiced. Releasing some of the held breath (especially if too much was taken in) may help to relax one. Overtensing certain muscles (occasionally between shots) fol-lowed by conscious efforts to "let them go" will tend to relax those muscles.

7. *Aiming*—There are three main methods of aiming: (1) Bare bow shooting without the use of any aiming device was used thousands of years ago and is now commonly called "instinctive shooting." This method will be explained later. (2) Hundreds of years ago target archers discovered they could shoot better scores by sighting the tips of their arrows onto an object on the ground, or elsewhere, and releasing without looking directly at the target. The object or aiming point was moved according to the grouping of arrows until it was known exactly where to place it so the arrows would strike the gold. This method was called *point-of-aim*. See Illustration 13.

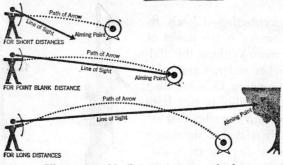

Illustration 13: Point-of-aim method

Point-of-aim is still used today in target archery but is not as convenient as the "sight method," and is losing its popularity. (3) The sight shooting method involves the use of a mechanical device, which is adjustable vertically and horizontally, attached to the bow. A sight may be purchased for as little as one dollar or as much as ten dollars or more and may be fastened securely to the bow with screws or tape. It may also consist of a popsicle stick held on with a few rubber bands, or a large-headed pin held by a piece of adhesive tape on the back of the bow. The principle of use is similar in either case. See Illustration 14.

The sight is usually fastened to the back of the bow about an inch above the arrow rest. The sight pin extends to the left side of the bow and is easily visible as it rides up and down the sight window. To aim with a sight, close the left eye (assuming the right eye is the master eye), and look at the sight pin and align it with the center of the gold. After shooting several arrows, check the group so that sight adjustments may be made. If the arrows are spread over the target there probably is inconsistency in performance rather than any fault with the sight's adjustment. Perfect form first till the arrows are grouping, then adjust the sight according to the group. To make sight adjustments follow this simple rule: *move the sight in the direction of the error.* If the group is high, move the pin up; if it is low, move the pin down. If the group is right, move the pin right; if it is left, move the pin left. All adjustments on the sight are made with the bow held as in the shooting position.

8. *Concentrating*—Closely related to aiming is the power of concentration. Without this ability an archer will not reach his peak performance. Concentrating involves the ability to cast from one's mind any thoughts that are not directly related to shooting a bow. Distracting thoughts may have a physical basis, such as soreness or tiredness; or they may be caused externally, by the wind, sun, or terrain; there may be emotional problems such as worry

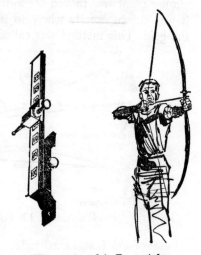

Illustration 14: Bow sights

over examinations, disagreements with others, or concern over finances; or the distraction may have a social basis, such as awareness of being watched by others or concern over finishing when the others do. The archer must devote his entire power of concentration to the sight and center of the target. All else should be forgotten. This ability to concentrate will not be possible, however, if the archer has to think about form. Consequently, form must first be perfected; it must become a habit. Think about form corrections between shots, not during the act of shooting.

9. *Releasing*—Releasing or loosing is the last act in shooting; without a good release, all the preceding actions are worthless. When the archer is relaxed in the full draw position, the sight pin is held steadily on the center of the target, and all powers of concentration

are focused on the task at hand, it is time to release. The archer releases by relaxing the string fingers smoothly, allowing the string to slide over the ends of the glove. Before and after the string is released there should be no voluntary movements of the string hand—that is, the hand should not be snapped to the side, jerked back, or allowed to creep forward. Mistakes in the release are caused by unnecessary movements before the string is actually gone from the fingers or arrows have left the bow completely.

10. *Follow-through*—The purpose of the follow-through is to ensure the effectiveness of proper fundamentals up to that point. *Follow-through* means merely holding form for a short time after release. Once the arrow has left the bow, the archer has no effect on its flight; but until the arrow is gone, the archer affects it, especially through his grip and bow arm movements. Some pointers on follow-through are: keep the anchor point positioned as during release; keep the bow arm extended to the target without allowing the arm to drop or move sideways, or the wrist to twist; maintain the shooting position at least until the arrow hits the target or a little longer, during which time the shot can be studied for correct fundamentals. The follow-through in archery may be likened to the "hold" after firing a rifle. The rifle is held on the target for a brief time after the shot is squeezed off and the shot is "called."

SHOOTING ERRORS

Regardless of who the archer is there probably will come a time when his score will decrease, often because of erratic form. Often the individual does not know what mistakes he is making. However, careful self-study or observation by another may soon reveal the answer to the problem. The following factors are listed as the most common shooting errors and some of their causes:

Error—shooting to the left

Causes:

1. Natural tendency of most bows to shoot to the left because of their construction. Center shot bows are less likely to do this.

2. Arrows spined too stiffly for the bow's weight.

3. Sighting with the left eye while shooting right-handed. Close the left eye and use the right.

4. Shooting right-handed but having the left eye as the master eye. Shoot left-handed if the left eye is the master eye and right-handed if the right eye is the master eye.

5. Sight pin being set too far to the right.

6. Hunching the bow arm shoulder. Keep the shoulder down and back.

7. Anchoring to the right of the proper anchor point.

8. Jerking the bow to the left on or before release.

9. Twisting the bow hand outward on or before release, causing the bow to turn left.

10. Left wrist not straight but turned in, causing bow to be angled off to the left.

11. Locking the bow arm too stiffly and tensely.

12. Snapping the bow string off to the right on release. Hold anchor.

13. Wind blowing from the right.

Error—shooting to the right

Causes:

1. Arrow spined too lightly for the bow.

2. Anchoring to the left of the correct position.

3. Bending the bow arm on or before release. Keep the arm straight.

4. Sight pin setting too far to the left.

5. Wind blowing from the left.

6. Outward wrist movement in bow arm on or before release.

Error—shooting too high

Causes:

1. Arrow being nocked below the correct nocking point.

2. Opening mouth before or during the release (thus lowering the anchor point).

3. Overdrawing (pulling beyond the normal anchor point).

4. Jerking hand back on release, resulting in extra cast.

5. Anchoring lower than normal anchor point.

6. Sight pin setting too low.

7. Leaning back (away from target) on or before release.

8. Overstrung bow (may result in greater cast).

9. Raising bow arm on or before release.
10. Tail wind.
11. Not breathing properly, inhaling just before release.

Error—shooting too low.

Causes:

1. Not drawing back to correct anchor point (underdrawing).
2. Letting string hand move forward on or before release (creeping).
3. Pushing or dropping bow arm down on or before release.
4. Arrow nocked above the correct nocking point—nock at a ninety-degree angle.
5. Collapsing the bow arm on or before release (loss of cast).
6. Not holding breath properly, exhaling just before release (thus lowering bow arm).
7. Anchoring too high.
8. Holding too long, possibly tiring and letting the bow arm settle slightly.
9. Leaning forward (toward the target) on or before release.
10. Setting sight pin falsely high.
11. Arrows too heavy for bow (loss of speed).
12. Bow too weak (poor cast for longer distances).
13. Bow understrung (loss of efficiency).
14. Hitting clothing, bow arm, or arm guard with the string upon release.
15. Head wind.

Combinations of these errors may cause arrows to hit high and right, for example, or low and left, or any other place on the target. On the other hand, one error might nullify the effect of another and result in a perfect shot. This should not be the archer's goal—to learn to use compensating errors. He should strive to perfect his form and shoot consistently correctly.

THE TEN TECHNIQUES OF BARE BOW SHOOTING

Bare bow shooting is commonly called *instinctive shooting,* which implies that this ability is somehow inborn in an individual. In reality this is far from the truth; the ability to shoot with this method is more dependent upon one's judgment than on instinct. It is a learned ability and a practiced judgment. For lack of a better name we will call this method the *bare bow method*, because in contrast to the other main method of shooting, the sight method, there is no aiming device whatever on the archer's bow, nor does he use a point of aim. Consequently, this method is primarily used for hunting since sight shooters must know distance to set their sights properly and hunting conditions do not lend themselves to the setting of sights. In addition to hunting, and of course bow fishing, bare bow shooting is used in field archery, which is a game designed to condition and train one for hunting. However, it must be realized at the outset that sights can be used very effectively in field archery and satisfactorily in hunting. Many people shoot both ways and it is highly advisable to learn both ways well and eventually to pick the method preferred. Also at times an archer sours on one method if used exclusively and will find freshness if he takes up the other style for a time. Both methods have advantages and disadvantages and it is up to the individual finally to judge for himself as to his preference.

The author has conducted research on several occasions and concluded that best results are obtained in the learning process by beginning with sight shooting and later learning bare bow shooting. The students who began shooting with sights shot higher scores on the first round and made greater improvements between rounds than did those students who started shooting using bare bow techniques. Also when the groups were switched the students who began shooting with sights immediately learned the bare bow style and made good progress while the others had some difficulty in adjusting to the sights and did not improve as rapidly.

It must be pointed out that for a high score, the sight method is superior. This is easily seen in the scores of archers who shoot in the national tournaments. Shooting on the same courses, the free style archers, who use sights, always outshoot the bare bow shooters—even in field archery competition, which is a game especially designed for and by bare bow archers.

There are a few differences in form between sight and bare bow shooting. The main differences are in aiming and anchor point. Since the techniques of shooting have been described under sight shooting they will only be listed here, but where major differences exist the differences will be explained.

1. *Stance*

    a. Stand relaxed at right angles to the target.
    b. In field archery stand behind the shooting post.
    c. Feet should be shoulder-width apart, weight evenly distributed.

2. *Grip and bow arm*

    a. Use the extended wrist grip if the bow is not too heavy, otherwise use the traditional grip (see Illustration 15).

    b. Align the bones to form a straight line through the wrist.
    c. Do not allow the wrist to move before, during, or just after release.
    d. Extend the bow arm fully.
    e. Turn the elbow outward.
    f. Keep the shoulder down and back.
    g. Tilt the bow slightly to the right to get a better view of the target and better eye alignment.

3. *Nocking*

    a. Nock about ⅜ inch above a right angle of the string and top of the arrow rest.

4. *Drawing*

    a. Place string in front of the first joint of the first three fingers and let it slip to the tips of the three fingers as far as possible without losing control.

Illustration 15: Traditional Grip

    b. Use the back, shoulder, and upper arm muscles in the draw; spread the arms.
    c. Take in a breath of air during the draw and hold it.
    d. Begin aiming during the draw. Look intently at the center of the target or a spot on the animal and begin pointing the bow at the intended target.

5. *Anchoring*

a. Consistently anchor exactly at the same place.

b. Anchor at the back corner of the mouth with the second fingertip and with the hand on the side of the cheek (see Illustration 16). The anchor point is raised from under the chin (as in sight shooting) to the cheek to get the arrow closer to the eye to provide a better feeling of sighting down the arrow (like a gun) when aiming. This higher anchor point also places the arrow directly *under* the right eye, which helps in aligning the arrow on the target. The head should be tilted slightly to the right to ensure having the right eye directly over the arrow. At the same time the bow should be tilted to the right somewhere between fifteen and thirty-five degrees (a matter of preference) to get a clearer view of the target and to have better eye alignment. Some archers prefer to keep the bow in the vertical position.

This anchor point is best secured if emphasis (pressure, firmness) is put on the position of the thumb and top of the index finger rather than on the fingertips. The first check point in anchoring is the position of the second finger. It should be placed at

Illustration 16: Anchoring

the back corner of the mouth tugging the lips back slightly as it comes to rest securely but not tightly. The thumb and index finger, which form a "V," should fit around the back of the cheekbone and should be firmly pressed against the cheek to disallow any movements. It is emphasized that pressure against the cheek should be applied with the upper parts of the index finger and thumb rather than with the fingertips. With the hand in this position another easily identifiable check point is the position of the top knuckle of the thumb. It comes to rest comfortably at the ear lobe. The archer should not release the arrow until the three check points are satisfactorily obtained, namely, the second finger at the back corner of the mouth, the "V" firmly around the cheekbone, and the top knuckle of the thumb at the ear lobe.

c. Anchor at the exact spot consistently. People with slightly varying facial characteristics may have to vary slightly from the suggested anchor point.

6. Relaxing

a. Take in a breath of air during the draw and hold it.
b. If too much air is inhaled release some.
c. Settle down at full draw. Relax musculature in legs and arms. Rest on the bones of the body.
d. Consciously relax the musculature of the body.

7. Aiming

Aiming while shooting with a bare bow is quite a departure from using a bow sight. Keep both eyes open rather than close the left eye. This affords a better perspective view, a bigger field of vision, and better depth perception. In other words, the target will be seen more clearly and the distance to the target will be judged more accurately. Occasionally, however, there will be an individual who will be better off to close one eye because of some peculiar characteristic of his vision.

The difficulty of shooting bare bow lies in the fact that every shot taken takes 100 per cent effort and concentration, there are no mechanical aids, no formulas, no sure-fire techniques. Each shot is an end in itself and if the archer cannot give his all he usually fails unless luck is with him.

The first important point in bare bow aiming is to *pick a spot* at which to aim. On the standard field archery target the center spot is well defined and quite small. On the standard target archery face, however, the gold center is large (9 inches), and at short distances (up to 40 yards) the exact center of the gold should be aimed at to focus the eyes on something small. In game hunting a spot must be selected on the animal (usually the heart area) to avoid looking at the entire animal. It is extremely important to be able to pick a focusing spot on any target. During the draw, begin to look at the spot; at full draw, with the arrow anchored properly under the right eye, concentrate intensely on the spot. Intently stare, think, and focus on the spot only; see in the field of vision secondarily the entire target, the bow, arrow, and bow arm. Do not look directly at any of the things that are in the field of vision—only at the exact spot to be hit. By looking at the intended target, the archer points the bow automatically at it, just as if he were pointing the index finger at something that the eyes are looking at. It is not necessary to look at the finger when pointing at something—only at the object. This process can also be compared to throwing a ball. The thrower looks only at the target (the glove or whatever) and throws to it without actually looking at his hand or the ball. He learns by practicing how low or high, or how hard or easy to deliver the ball. This is exactly what the bare bow archer must learn to do. He needn't be concerned with how hard or easy to shoot (because each shot should be the same full draw), but he needs to learn how high or low to aim depending on the distance to the target. This is the difficult part of bare bow shooting. It must be learned through practice and understanding of the equipment being used. Naturally, the longer distances afford the most difficulty in making the elevation adjustment. At long distances, hold the bow hand above the target; at short distances, hold the hand below the target. There is no rule to state how high or low to hold. It depends on the bow's weight, the arrows, the anchor point, and other such variables. If arrows are grouping on the target in a vertical line pattern it indicates that releases are good but that difficulty is being encountered in elevation judgment. If arrows are spread laterally, it may indicate good elevation judgment, but poor releases, bow hand movements, or other form mistakes.

It is known that many bare bow archers look at the distance relationship between their arrow tip and the center of the target or some other part of the target on long shots, or aim the arrow tip above the center (as is done in point-of-aim) instead of looking only at the center of the target. This then becomes a point-of-aim method of shooting. Pure instinctive or bare bow shooters do not employ these or other mechanical aiming techniques.

8. *Concentrating*

If the fundamentals of shooting bare bow style are mastered, concentration becomes the most important aspect of shooting. The importance of the ability to focus on a spot and forget everything else cannot be overemphasized. Look at the spot so intently as to become nearly self-hypnotized. Upon release the arrow slips away and seems to fly down a tube which is pointed at mid-center. Both eyes must be trained to focus unwaveringly at a small spot (in the case of a rabbit sitting at three yards it may be a certain hair near the heart area), nothing must be allowed to interfere with the shot at hand, not even thinking about getting a smooth release. Form must be automatic before intense concentration is possible. In the final analysis an archer will probably become as skilled as his concentration powers permit. This presupposes that form is perfected and good equipment is used.

9. Releasing

a. Let the string slip off the ends of the fingers.
b. Do not make any movements before, during, or after release that may affect the flight of the arrow.
c. The "dead" release is recommended—do not let the hand slide back on release. The sliding release may be permissible for experts, but it seems to be too difficult for beginners.

10. Follow-through

a. Maintain the anchor point for a few moments after release.
b. Keep the bow arm extended and pointing at the target for a few moments after release.
c. Do not let the wrist of the bow arm twist before, during, or after release.
d. Study the shot—why was it good or bad?
e. If any mistakes were made in form, implant the proper way of doing it in mind before the next shot. Think the correct way of shooting and then do it that way on the next shot.

RULES

The rules pertaining to archery may be divided into two categories, those dealing with safety of personnel or equipment and those concerned with competition or participation. Since there is an element of danger in the use of bows and arrows the safety rules should be strictly kept. If they are, the sport will be perfectly safe and enjoyable for all concerned.

SAFETY RULES AND PRECAUTIONS

1. Do not draw a bow without an arrow in it. This may result in overdrawing since the arrow is not present to act as a guide to indicate proper draw length, and the bow may break.
2. Never release the bowstring without an arrow on it. The shock sometimes breaks the bow or the string.
3. Limber a bow up with several short draws before pulling it to full draw. This is especially important if the bow has been idle for some time or if the temperature is radically different from that in which the bow was stored.
4. Check to see that the proper distance exists between the bow handle and string. This distance is a *fistmele*, or that distance recommended by the manufacturer. Make adjustments as necessary by taking the string off the bow and twisting or untwisting it. Too little distance results in wrist slap, too great a distance may result in a broken bow. Neither is good for the bow's efficiency.
5. Check arrows before shooting for cracks, chrysals, splinters, loose feathers, loose nocks or points, glue deposits, and for straightness. Do not shoot damaged arrows.
6. Be sure arrows are long enough. Never draw an arrow past the bow handle between string and belly. If the correct length cannot be had, it is safer to have slightly longer arrows rather than shorter ones.

7. Check the bow for chrysals, cracks, splits, or scratches, and determine beforehand if there is danger of breakage.

8. Check the string before shooting for frays, broken strands, and loose serving. Repair or replace the string before breakage occurs.

9. Don't bend a bow backward. It is designed and built to bend one way only.

10. When carrying equipment to or on the archery range, carry bows in the vertical position and arrows by the "piles" or tips, spreading them apart so that the feathers are separated.

11. Never shoot an arrow straight up in the air. This is very dangerous and the arrow often goes out of sight and wind currents affect it, making it extremely difficult to know where the arrow will hit when it lands.

12. Never point an "armed" bow at a person.

13. Wear simple clothing. Avoid fancy buttons, big pockets, jewelry, beads, sorority pins, fraternity pins, and so on, because the bowstring often catches on such things, and the arrow is deflected, or jewelry may be pulled off by the string and lost.

14. Keep the bow arm elbow turned out to avoid hitting it with the bowstring.

15. Be sure to wear an arm guard and finger tab or glove. Welts or blisters may develop without this needed protection.

16. Do not shoot if anyone is at the target, behind the target, or between the archer and the target.

17. When pulling arrows from the target, have everyone cleared away from the immediate front of the target to avoid the possibility of accident as the arrows are removed. Serious injury to the eyes of others could result during the arrow withdrawal process.

18. To withdraw the arrow, place one hand against the target, palm out, with the arrow between the first and second fingers; with the other hand grasping the arrow close to the target, pull the arrow out at the same angle it went in.

19. When arrows become buried in the grass, pull them forward from the pile end to avoid feather damage.

20. Arrows with feathers partially driven into the target should be pulled through from behind the target pile first.

21. Always be conscious of the possible danger of bows and arrows. The bow should be treated as a lethal weapon.

SIMPLIFIED RULES OF COMPETITION AND PARTICIPATION IN TARGET ARCHERY

1. Straddle the shooting line.
2. Wait for a signal from the field captain when to begin shooting.
3. Shoot six arrows only.
4. Step back three paces after shooting an end.
5. Wait for a signal from the field captain when to retrieve arrows.
6. All archers shoot at the same time and retrieve at the same time.
7. In target archery, shoot only at the target.
8. An arrow that falls from the bow that can be reached with the aid of the bow may be shot again. If it can't be reached without moving, it is considered shot and counts zero.
9. If tackle breaks during shooting, the arrow is considered shot.
10. Six arrows constitute an "end." A round is made up of a number of ends at several (usually three) different ranges (or distances).

Illustration 17: The target

11. Score—the target (see Illustration 17) consists of five concentric rings. The yellow inner ring (gold) counts nine points; the red counts seven; the blue five; the black three; and the white one.
12. An arrow that cuts a line between two colors counts the higher value.
13. An arrow that passes through the scoring face so that it is not visible from the front shall count seven at 60 yards or less, and five for ranges beyond 60 yards. Arrows passing completely through the target, if witnessed, are scored in the same manner.

14. An arrow that hits in the petticoat has no scoring value. The petticoat includes the outer black line around the white ring and the area outside of this ring.

15. An arrow that rebounds from the scoring face, if witnessed, shall score the same as a pass-through.

16. An arrow that hits a target other than the one shot at shall score as a miss.

17. If more than six arrows are shot in one end, only the lowest six shall score.

18. In tournament shooting, usually groups of four people shoot at each target. One is the target captain who calls the value of each arrow as he pulls it from the target. Its value shall be recorded independently by two contestants acting as scorers, normally the next two assigned to the target. Scorers should check results after each end to avoid errors. Each archer is individually responsible for seeing that his arrows are called correctly and entered properly on the score card.

19. Scores are recorded by listing the highest first and proceeding to the lowest. Each score must be recorded in the space provided on the scoring card. Zero is indicated for misses or hits outside the scoring face.

20. The longest distance in a round is shot first, progressing to the shortest.

21. In case of a tie, the highest score at the longest distance is the winner.

22. In a tournament, there is no practice allowed between the various ranges which constitute the round.

23. The center of the gold should be 4 feet from the ground.

24. An arrow must be left in the target until scored.

25. Arrows must bear a distinctive crest so that they can be identified easily.

26. If the point-of-aim method of shooting is used, the aiming point may not be placed more than 6 inches above the ground.

27. Any type of bow except a crossbow may be used in competition. Crossbow enthusiasts often stage separate tournaments.

28. Presiding officials in tournaments are the *Field Captain* for men and the *Lady Paramount* for ladies.

29. Classifications of archers:

> Men
> Women
> Intermediate boys and girls (fifteen to seventeen years old)
> Junior boys and girls (twelve to fourteen years old)
> Beginner boys and girls, or Cadets (eleven years and under)

30. Some of the commonly used rounds include:

A. The Columbia Round—for women, intermediate girls, and junior girls (this round works well for college men beginners, and could be used for high school boys):

> four ends at 50 yards;
> four ends at 40 yards;
> four ends at 30 yards.

B. The American Round—for men and women, intermediate boys and girls:

> five ends at 60 yards;
> five ends at 50 yards;
> five ends at 40 yards.

C. The National Round—for women and intermediate girls:

> eight ends at 60 yards;
> four ends at 50 yards.

D. The Metropolitan Round—for women:

> five ends at 60 yards;
> five ends at 50 yards;
> five ends at 40 yards;
> five ends at 30 yards.

E. The Metropolitan Round—for men:

> five ends at 100 yards;
> five ends at 80 yards;
> five ends at 60 yards;
> five ends at 50 yards;
> five ends at 40 yards.

F. The York Round—for men (one of the oldest):

> twelve ends at 100 yards;
> eight ends at 80 yards;
> four ends at 60 yards.

G. Junior Columbia—for junior girls or all beginners under twelve:

> four ends at 40 yards;
> four ends at 30 yards;
> four ends at 20 yards.

H. Junior American—for junior boys:

> five ends at 50 yards;
> five ends at 40 yards;
> five ends at 30 yards.

I. Junior Metropolitan—for juniors:

> five ends at 40 yards;
> five ends at 30 yards;
> five ends at 20 yards.

J. Cadet American—for boys and girls under eleven years:

> fifteen arrows at 30 yards;
> fifteen arrows at 20 yards.

31. For further information on tournaments or interpretations of rules consult the National Archery Association, Secretary-Treasurer, Mrs. Helen Huck, 20-A Yale Avenue, Buffalo 26, New York.

SIMPLIFIED RULES FOR FIELD ARCHERY

1. Archers shoot in groups of four. One is the target captain who pulls the arrows and calls the score while the scorer records the scores.

2. The course should be so constructed that it is safe to be shooting at all targets simultaneously without endangering any of the participants.

3. The danger signal is "timber."

4. Be courteous while others shoot. No loud talking or distracting incidences should take place to bother other competitors.

5. Stand behind the shooting stake when addressing the target and shoot four arrows at the target if it is a one-position shot. If it is a four-position shot, shoot one arrow from each position. The

four positions may be either a fan-shape or a walk-up type, which gets progressively closer to the target on each shot.

6. If archers are looking for stray arrows behind the target one archer should remain at the target or a bow should be left standing across the target face. The succeeding archers should not shoot until all archers have safely left for the next target.

7. Scoring—The center circle of white including the small black spot scores five while the outer black circle counts three. See Illustration 18.

Arrows that bisect a line count the higher value. Arrows that penetrate through the target face so the nocks are not visible from the front score three. Each score must be recorded on the score sheet with the highest scores first. All misses are listed as zeros.

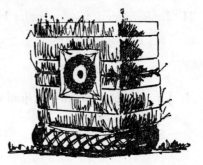

Illustration 18: Field archery target

8. The Flint Round is recommended for beginners. See Table 5–1 for the course set-up.

TABLE 5-1

Course Set-up for the Flint Round

Target 1	25 yards	12-inch face
Target 2	20 feet	6-inch face
Target 3	30 yards	12-inch face
Target 4	15 yards	6-inch face
Target 5	20 yards	12-inch face
Target 6	10 yards	6-inch face
Target 7	30, 25, 20, 15 yards (walk-up, one shot from each post)	12-inch face

9. For course construction, club formation, or interpretation of rules concerning field archery consult the National Field Archery Association, Post Office Box H, Palm Springs, California.

Other Archery Games

1. *Archery Golf*

In some parts of the country archery golf is a popular game. It is played on a golf course. One bow and three arrows may be used: the flight arrow, the approach arrow, and the putting arrow. The cup is a 4-inch disc or ball placed near the green cup. The object of the game is to go around the course in as few shots as possible. Nine under golf par for nine holes is considered good archery golf par. The game may easily be improvised for any large open area and could be played most of the year around.

2. *Wand Shooting*

This game consists of shooting thirty-six arrows at a wand 2 inches wide and 6 feet above the ground. Balsa wood is best because it holds arrows and minimizes rebounds. Men shoot from 100 yards and women from 60 yards. The wand or stripe could be made of paper and put on a regular target and the distances could be modified. Only those arrows count as hits which are actually embedded in the wand, or which are witnessed rebounds.

3. *Clout Shooting*

Clouts consists of shooting at a 48-foot-diameter target laid out on the ground in concentric circles like a 48-inch target, with like values for scoring. Thirty-six arrows are shot from 180 yards for men; women shoot the same number of arrows from 140 or 120 yards. A flag is used to mark the center of the target.

4. *Roving Archery*

Rovers consists of picking targets at random. Each archer shoots one shot. A direct hit or the closest to a hit scores one point. The point winner selects the next target. Distances are varied and targets may include clumps of grass, stumps, paper, and so on. The player with the highest number of points is the winner.

6 TRAINING PROGRAM

It is well known to all athletes that they must train to achieve success in their sports. Likewise in archery, a type of training program must be pursued, whether to become highly skilled or merely to learn to shoot properly. The following outline suggests a type of program that could be followed by an instructor teaching a course in target archery or by an individual who wishes to learn to shoot, but does not have the help of a qualified instructor. The outline will be set up for twenty one-hour periods of actual participation but it will be presupposed that additional time will be spent in reading and studying archery materials.

Whenever the outline says to review or analyze something the individual should restudy by rereading the material presented earlier. If an instructor is available he should verbally review and demonstrate whenever possible.

A TARGET ARCHERY TRAINING PROGRAM

1. Equipment should be purchased and fitted to the individual. The bow should not be too heavy and the arrows should be matched to the bow. All equipment should be safe and in good repair. Targets should be available (bales of excelsior or straw are fine), but it is not necessary to use target faces to begin with; the emphasis should be placed on the development of form, not on the score shot. Study stringing the bow and practice this several times until it becomes easy. Study the techniques of shooting, especially stance, grip, draw, anchor, and release. Begin shooting at the target from a 10-yard distance, merely aiming at the center of the target (without face) and getting the feel of the draw, of the muscles being used, of the stability of the stance, and especially of the anchor point.

2. Review form or the techniques of shooting. Study carefully the grip, the anchor point, and the release. Shoot at 10 yards, trying to

do everything perfectly and consistently. Study and analyze strengths and weaknesses. Review any portions of the fundamentals that are not clear. Shoot again, constantly thinking about the correct way of shooting.

3. Review all the techniques of shooting, paying particular heed to releasing the grip and aiming. Begin shooting at 20 yards, using the point-of-aim method. It is valuable to know how to shoot this way even though it may not be selected as the final way to shoot. Line the aiming point (a white block of wood) up between the target and archer, sight the tip of the arrow (at full draw), hold it on the aiming point, and release. Shoot several arrows and check the group. If the arrows are grouped the aiming point may be moved (move it in the direction the arrows should go) so the arrows group in the center of the target. Continue shooting and reviewing form. Try to have all or most of the arrows hit in a 12-inch-diameter circle. Be consistent in form, but be consistently right.

4. Review form—especially anchoring, releasing, gripping, and aiming. Place a sight on the bow, either manufactured or homemade of a coffee stick and rubber band. Put a small piece of paper (about 6 inches square) in the center of the target to aim at. From a distance of 20 yards, shoot at the piece of paper, using the bow sight. If arrows are grouping, adjust the sight pin so the group hits the paper. If arrows are spread, study the fundamentals again and analyze mistakes. Try to perfect form. Results at the target are nearly automatic if form is perfected.

5. Review aiming, releasing, and grip and bow arm fundamentals. Shoot from 30 yards at a standard 48-inch target face. Use the sight, be concerned with arrow grouping, and adjust the sight to be able to hit consistently well. Toward the end of the session, count the score on several ends. If end scores are around thirty or more, good progress is being made. If scores are very low or arrows are not grouping, analyze form and make corrections. At the end of the period, mark the pin setting for the 30-yard distance.

6. Review releasing, bow arm fundamentals, and aiming. Shoot an end or two from the 30-yard distance for review practice. Move to the 40-yard range and adjust the sight accordingly. At the end of the period mark the sight setting for 40 yards. Analyze the mistakes in form, think about the correct procedures.

7. Review fundamentals; put special emphasis on relaxation, concentration, and follow-through. Shoot two ends from the 40-yard range as review. Move back to 50 yards, adjust the pin setting down to allow for a higher trajectory. Be very careful about holding a steady bow arm, check the grip, relax on each shot, concentrate on the center of the target, and follow through. After shooting at 50 yards, mark the pin setting for future reference. The sight settings should now be marked for 50, 40, and 30 yards.

8. Study the rules of tournament shooting. Use a score card (found in Chapter 8) and begin shooting a Columbia Round—four ends at 50 yards, four at 40, and four at 30. If the round cannot be completed in one period, continue it the next time.

9. Finish the first Columbia Round, if necessary, and begin the second Columbia Round. Plot Columbia Round scores on Table 8–5, Chapter 8. Review any portion of form that seems to need it before beginning the second round. Analyze form, make adjustments when needed, try to be perfect in techniques.

10. Finish the second Columbia Round if necessary. Check the round score made against the standards in Chapter 8. If score is high, form is probably good and with more diligent practice and desire you could become a fine archer. If score is low, perhaps form is still not mastered, some mistakes are being made, and the techniques should be studied further and more effort should be made to correct the fundamentals. Finish the period by practicing without keeping score.

11. Study the techniques of bare bow shooting in Chapter 4. Begin shooting with this method at 20 yards. Pay special heed to the anchor point, release, and grip and bow arm fundamentals. Shoot several ends at 20 yards, move back to 30 yards to finish the period. Analyze form, make corrections when necessary.

12. Review bare bow form. Study very carefully the anchor point, release, grip, aiming, concentrating, and follow-through. Shoot several ends at 30 yards, move to 40 yards for several ends, then to 50 yards. Analyze form throughout.

13. Review the techniques of aiming, concentrating, and follow-through very precisely. Begin a Columbia Round using bare bow techniques.

14. Review aiming, concentrating, and following through. Finish

the first bare bow Columbia Round, if necessary. Start the second Columbia Round. Think constantly about performing fundamentals correctly.

15. Finish the second bare bow Columbia Round, if necessary. Complete the period by shooting bare bow style, varying the range constantly after each end, that is, at 20, 60, 30, 50, and 40 yards.

16. Play archery golf (see Chapter 5 for rules). Have fun.

17. Shoot a Flint Round (score cards in Chapter 8) on the target range or on a field range adapted for outdoor use. See Chapter 5 for rules of field archery and the set-up for the Flint Round.

18. Play rovers. See Chapter 5 for roving archery rules.

19. Shoot a final Columbia Round using either the sight or bare bow method. Most archers will find they get better scores using the sight.

20. Finish the Columbia Round, if necessary, and evaluate form using the Archery Form Evaluation Checklist found in Table 8-1, Chapter 8. Answer the Archery Knowledge Questions in Table 8-2. These evaluations will aid in determining amount of learning. Compare the best Columbia Round score with those in Table 8-3, or the Flint Round scores on Table 8-4. Plot the Columbia Round scores on Table 8-5 to check individual progress.

With this type of training as a background the archer should have developed an interest in the sport and a fair degree of proficiency. No one will be a champion at this stage of the game. This takes considerably more practice. The ground work has now been laid, however, so enjoy the sport and above all participate for a lifetime. The skill is yours.

A FIELD AND HUNTING ARCHERY TRAINING PROGRAM

This training program, of twenty one-hour periods, may be used as a guide for the instructor or for the individual who wishes to learn to shoot with the bare bow method or to prepare himself for bow hunting for deer.

1. After having carefully selected equipment, study bow stringing and practice it several times. Study the techniques of bare bow shooting. Begin shooting at 10 yards without using target faces. Try to pick a spot on the target to shoot at. Review the anchor point and the bow grip

2. Review form fundamentals, emphasis on anchor, release, and grip. Shoot at 10 yards. Analyze form and study the fundamentals once more. Move to 15 yards for several hands (a hand is four arrows.

3. Start shooting at 15 yards (no target face). Review form—anchor, release, grip and bow arm, and aiming. Analyze the techniques employed and try correcting any deviations from accepted form. Move to 20 yards to finish the period.

4. Study very carefully aiming, concentrating, and following through. Try to do the exact, fundamentally right thing on each shot. Shoot from 20 yards, using field faces. Analyze form, then move to 25 yards.

5. Review form, especially releasing, aiming, concentrating, and following through. Shoot several hands from 25 yards and move back to 30 yards to finish the period.

6. Shoot a Flint Round (rules in Chapter 5). Analyze form throughout. Results at the target are usually commensurate with the form of the archer. Plot Flint Round scores on Table 8–6, Chapter 8.

7. Shoot a second Flint Round. Refer to the standards found in Chapter 8 for an indication of progress. If score is low, perhaps more study and effort is necessary to perfect the techniques of shooting. If score is high it is indicative either of good progress, good form, good ability, or all of these. Keep up the good work. Constantly make the effort to improve. Success breeds success; success usually means lifelong participation.

8. Play archery golf (see rules in Chapter 5).

9. Play rovers (rules in Chapter 5).

10. Shoot at moving targets. Targets may be run back and forth on pulley arrangements or they may be dragged across by another person using a long (100-foot) rope. The latter type of target might be a gunny sack filled with leaves or straw. Vary the range and the speed of the moving target to simulate actual hunting conditions.

11. Shoot from a moving canoe or boat at target placed along the shore (if water is available). If no water is available, shoot at moving targets or play rovers.

12. Shoot a third Flint Round after reviewing form fundamentals.

13. Shoot a round on an NFAA field course (targets range from 20 feet to 80 yards in distance and from 6 to 24 inches in diameter).

If no field course is available, shoot the longer distances (60 to 80 yards) at the larger targets (18 and 24 inches), at any suitable location.

14. Go rabbit hunting or carp shooting (or any other type of game) if at all possible.

15. Study or discuss deer hunting. Emphasis on: what they eat and when; where they sleep and when. Discuss deer senses—smell, hearing, eyesight. Study or discuss how to hunt them, taking deer senses into consideration. How to locate feeding areas, bedding areas, and runways should be discussed. Tips on how to move into the wind, move quietly, move slowly, wear appropriate clothing, and how to construct blinds should be studied.

16. Review form and shoot a fourth Flint Round.

17. Start at 20 feet and shoot constantly from that distance until success is achieved, then move to 10 yards. Shoot at each distance long enough to ensure mastery and move back 5 yards at a time. Mastery might be considered the ability to hit a hand in the five score or a hand of no target misses (all shots are hits).

18. Continue the process of shooting at a certain distance until that distance is mastered before moving back. Review concentration and follow-through.

19. Shoot a fifth Flint Round.

20. Evaluate form using the Archery Form Evaluation Checklist, Table 8–1 in Chapter 8. Compare best Flint Round scores with those in Table 8–3 and plot all Flint Round scores in Table 8–6 to check the progress made.

After this training session, the archer should be interested in continuing the sport, have a reasonable degree of skill, and be ready to pursue the deer. Good luck. Don't give up after an unsuccessful season, for you may get a big one next year. This challenging sport is yours; use it for life.

7

GLOSSARY

This glossary will include only those terms being currently used. It is not intended to include every term that has had significance in the field of archery.

Arm guard: A device worn on the forepart of the bow arm to protect the arm and wrist from the slap and recoil of the bowstring.

Arrow rest: The part of the bow handle or bow that forms a shelf to hold the arrow as it rides across the bow.

Back: The flat side of a bow which is away from the archer as he is shooting; the part of the bow that is most under tension during the draw.

Backed bow: A bow that has been strengthened or protected by some material glued to the back, such as rawhide, wood with high tensile strength, Fiberglas, bamboo, or metal.

Belly: The inside of the bow facing the archer as he is shooting; the part of the bow that is compressed during the draw.

Bending the bow, bracing the bow, stringing the bow: Terms used to describe the process of placing the bowstring into the bow notches to ready it for shooting.

Blunt: An arrow with a blunt tip instead of a pointed one, used primarily for small-game hunting. The tip may be metal, rubber, or plastic.

Bowman: Another term for an archer, one who engages in shooting bows and arrows.

Bow stave: A piece of cut wood from which a bow is made.

Bowyer: A person who makes archery tackle, especially bows.

Broadhead: A tip used on hunting arrows; there are various designs, but all are essentially designed with sharp cutting edges to permit deep penetration to kill game by hemorrhage.

Butt or target: A backstop to halt arrows; it may be baled straw or excelsior, or round, woven targets of straw or grasses.

Cast: The ability of a bow to shoot an arrow; the distance a bow can shoot; or the speed at which the bow delivers arrows.

Chrysal: Compression fracture of fibers usually showing as a line across the belly of a self bow. Chrysals may be seen on arrows also, especially if they have been stepped on.

Clout shooting: Shooting at a 48-foot-diameter target laid out on the ground in concentric circles. Men shoot from 180 yards and women from 120 or 140 yards.

Cock feather: The feather at right angles to the nock. It should be perpendicular to the bow when the arrow is being shot.

Composite bow: A bow made of two or more materials, such as wood and Fiberglas.

Creep: To allow the string hand to move forward just before or during the release, resulting in a loss of cast.

Crest: Colored marks on the arrow used for identification.

Draw, pull, spread: The act of pulling the bowstring the proper distance, to the anchor point. *Draw* and *pull* also refer to the act of removing the arrows from the target.

End: Six arrows shot in succession.

Eye, loop: The bend in the ends of a bowstring to secure it to the bow.

Field arrow: An arrow used mostly in field archery. It is usually more rugged than a target arrow, having bigger vanes and a heavier, longer pile or tip.

Field captain: Man on the target range in charge of a tournament.

Finger tab, finger cot, finger stall, finger tip, finger glove: Leather device used for the three shooting or string fingers to protect them from the bowstring and also to give a smoother release.

Fistmele: The distance between the base of the hand and the tip of the extended thumb (about 6 or 7 inches). It is the desired distance between the bow handle and the string and should be checked before using the bow each session. Follow the bow manufacturer's specifications whenever given.

Fletching: The feathers on an arrow, usually three or four.

Flight arrow: A long, thin, light arrow, usually barreled with small vanes and pile, used in distance shooting.

Flight shooting: Shooting an arrow for maximum distance. Arrows have been shot over one-half mile.

Follow the string: An expression used to explain the set a bow takes toward the string after being used. A good bow should not follow the string to any appreciable degree.

Footed arrow: An arrow that has a piece of hardwood spliced into the foreshaft to give it more weight, strength, and better balance.

Grip: The handle of a bow.

Ground quiver: A rod of metal stuck into the ground, shaped to hold arrows and bows while on the range.

Group: Arrows in the target in close proximity.

Hand: Shooting four arrows in field archery.

Head, tip, point, pile: The "business end" of the arrow, usually made of brass, steel, or aluminum.

Hen feathers: The two feathers on an arrow paralleling the nock.

Hit: A successful shot within the target scoring face.

Holding: Keeping an arrow at full draw while aiming. The hold should be for two or three seconds.

Instinctive shooting: Aiming and shooting a bow without the aid of a point of aim, bow sight, or other mechanical means. It is better described as a learned judgment rather than an instinct. Within this text it is called the *bare bow method* of shooting.

Jerking: Abruptly moving the string hand on release.

Kick: The recoil of a bow after it is shot.

Lady paramount: Woman on the range in charge of a tournament.

Limbs: The two arms of a bow, one above and one below the handle.

Longbow: A hand bow 5 or more feet in length.

Loose, release: The act of letting the string slip from the fingertips to shoot the arrow.

Nock: The groove on the end of an arrow into which the string fits.

Also the notches on either end of a bow which hold the string. To place an arrow on the string is "nocking an arrow."

Nocking point: The position on the string where the arrow is placed.

Overbowed: Using a bow that is too heavy for the individual.

Overdraw: To pull an arrow past the handle of the bow or to use a longer arrow than the bow was designed to handle safely.

Overstrung: The string being too short for the bow, more than a fistmele between bow handle and string.

Petticoat: The black rim and all the target face outside the white; an arrow in the petticoat counts as a miss.

Point-blank range: The distance at which the aiming point is at the center of the gold, while using the point-of-aim method of shooting.

Point-of-aim: A method of aiming using an aiming point to sight upon with the tip of the arrow to aid the archer in hitting the target.

Quiver: A receptacle for holding arrows. Types of quivers include: back, hip, bow, leg, arm, and ground.

Range: The distance to be shot; or the place where shooting is done.

Range finder: A device to aid the archer in relocating the position of his aiming point.

Recurved bow: A bow with tips that curve back in a graceful arc.

Reflexed bow: A bow that bends backward in its entirety when unstrung, but does not necessarily have recurved ends. Bows may be recurved and reflexed.

Release: To let the string slip off the fingertips; to shoot the arrow.

Round: Shooting a prescribed number of ends or hands at prescribed distances.

Roving: Shooting at random targets such as stumps, paper, clumps of grass, and so on, with unknown and varying distances; good practice for hunting.

Scattered: Describes arrows that are in different places on the target rather than grouped.

Self arrow: An arrow of a single piece of wood, in contrast to a footed arrow.

Self bow: A bow made of one kind of wood, in contrast to a composite bow.

Serving: The winding of string around the center of a bowstring and its loops to protect it from wear by the fingers, arrow nock, and bow nocks.

Shaft: The dowel of which an arrow is made.

Shaftment: That portion of the arrow from the nock through the crest.

Shooting line: The line the target archer straddles while shooting at targets.

Spine: The stiffness-flexibility combination of an arrow. Arrows should be spined for the weight of the bow in which they are used.

Stagger: The erratic flight of an arrow.

Tackle: The equipment used by an archer.

Target face: The painted part of a target including the gold and the other concentric rings.

Tassel: Cloth with which to wipe arrows that become wet or soiled.

Throwaways: Arrow no longer good for competition, but usable when chance of their being broken or lost is great.

Timber: Term used in field archery to warn others that an arrow is being shot; same as "fore" in golf.

Timber hitch: A kind of knot used to tie the lower end of a single-looped string to the bow.

Toxophilite: One who loves, studies, and practices archery.

Trajectory: The path of an arrow in flight.

Underbowed: Using a bow that is too light for the archer.

Understrung: Describes a bow having a string too long; less than a fistmele between handle and string.

Vane: Feather on an arrow.

Wand shooting: Shooting at a slat 2 inches wide and 6 feet high from a long distance.

Weight: The number of pounds pull required to pull a bow the correct arrow length. The actual weight of an arrow in grains.

Weight in hand: The avoirdupois weight of a bow.

Wobble: The erratic action of an arrow in flight.

SELF-TESTING AND EVALUATION

In archery, perhaps more so than in most sports, form plays a significant role. Often the archer is not aware of his own mistakes in form. Therefore, it is suggested that he work with an expert instructor, with an experienced archer, or analyze himself using the checklist that follows in Table 8–1. Better still, do all three.

TABLE 8-1

Archery Form Evaluation Checklist

Name of Archer _____ Date _____

Name of Evaluator _____ Type of Shooting _____

Check (√) each item if it is correctly executed. Mark it (X) if incorrect and note in the space provided what is wrong or what needs to be done to improve.

1. *Stance*

____A. Feet parallel, shoulder width apart. _____

____B. Weight evenly distributed (astride shooting line in target archery, behind post in field archery). _____

____C. Body erect, abdomen flat, weight supported by bones, relaxed. _____

2. *Grip and Bow Arm*

____A. Extended wrist grip used, relaxed fingers. _____

____B. Upper edge of index finger just below the arrow rest.

____C. Wrist straight. _____

____D. Elbow pointing outward, arm not locked. _____

____E. Shoulder level, not hunched or turned in. _____

____F. No wrist movement before, during, or immediately following the release. _____

____G. Bow arm steady. _____

3. *Nocking*

_____A. Arrow nocked consistently at a 90° angle with the string, bisecting at the arrow rest for sight shooting. Arrow nocked ⅜″ above a 90° angle for bare bow shooting. _____

_____B. Cock feather out. _____

4. *Drawing*

_____A. String gripped near the fingertips with three fingers. _____

_____B. *Fingers only* form a hook, hand is straight and relaxed, thumb in palm. _____

_____C. Forearm, wrist, and hand form a continuous line with the arrow. _____

_____D. Full draw on each shot. _____

_____E. Bow arm extended to target and draw completed simultaneously. _____

_____F. Relaxation evident. _____

_____G. Breath taken and held. _____

5. *Anchoring*

_____A. Anchor point (under chin for sight shooting; at corner of mouth for bare bow shooting) consistently the same. _____

_____B. String cuts across center of chin, lips, and nose in sight shooting, at side of nose in bare bow shooting. _____

_____C. Head remains level and turned fully toward the target. _____

_____D. Mouth closed, chin in normal position. _____

6. *Relaxing*

_____A. Body weight settled onto the bones rather than supported tensely by musculature. _____

_____B. Good breath control evident. _____

_____C. Conscious effort to relax musculature evident. _____

7. *Aiming*

_____A. Aim for two or three seconds *after* coming to full draw. _____

_____B. Left eye closed (for most archers) when using sight; both eyes open (for most archers) when bare bow shooting. _____

_____C. Eyes function properly, master eye is known. _____

8. *Concentrating*

____A. Archer seems to have mastered any physical or emotional problems and devotes all his attention to hitting the target. _____

____B. Form is perfected, so concentration can be obtained without the problem of trying to correct any aspect of form. _____

9. *Releasing*

____A. Anchor point remains solid before, during, and immediately after release. _____

____B. The string slips off the fingertips. _____

10. *Following through*

____A. No string hand movements that adversely affect the arrow's flight. _____

____B. No unwarranted grip and bow arm movements. _____

____C. Shooting position is held until the arrow hits the target.

KNOWLEDGE IN ARCHERY

The following questions in Table 8–2 should be answered to ensure a well-rounded knowledge of archery.

TABLE 8-2

Archery Knowledge Questions

1. What are the main types of woods used in making bows?
2. What woods are used in making arrows?
3. Name the parts of a bow.
4. Name the parts of an arrow.
5. How is arrow length determined?
6. What is meant by *spine*?
7. What is the size of an official target archery face? Give scoring values.
8. How many archers shoot at each target in a tournament? What are their titles and duties?
9. What is the title of the person in charge of a tournament?
10. What is meant by *cast*?
11. How is point-of-aim used?
12. What does *fistmele* mean?

13. How is the score recorded?
14. What does *creeping* mean?
15. What are the ten fundamental techniques of shooting? Describe each.
16. How is a bow sight used?
17. How is a single-looped bowstring attached to a bow?
18. What causes arrows to hit to the left?
19. What causes arrows to hit too low?
20. What are the safety rules in archery?

COLUMBIA AND FLINT ROUND STANDARDS

It is usually desirable to know how one's performance rates with that of others. Tables 8–3 and 8–4 give percentile rankings for the various scores made on Columbia and Flint Rounds by college men and women. If an archer's score falls in the ninetieth percentile it means that he is better than 90 per cent of the beginning male college archers. (It is assumed that the samples—265 cases of men on the Columbia and forty-six men and twenty-five women on the Flint—upon which the tables are based are typical of beginning college groups.) Likewise, if the score is at the tenth percentile, it means the archer is better than only 10 per cent of his peers.

TABLE 8-3

Percentile Scores for Men *
(Columbia Round Best Score)

Percentile Rank	Columbia Round Score
100	511
90	411
80	385
70	367
60	345
50	320
40	304
30	283
20	259
10	237
0	190

* Women could probably use this table by lowering each score by fifty points and be reasonably accurate.

TABLE 8-4

Field Archery Scores—Flint Round
(Percentile Rankings)

Men's Score	Percentile	Women's Score
155	100	70
115	90	53
90	80	46
85	70	32
77	60	30
68	50	26
59	40	25
55	30	15
43	20	12
29	10	9
20	0	3

PROFILE RECORD

Plot scores on Table 8–5 to check progress being made in target archery.

TABLE 8-5					
Profile Record of Columbia Round Scores					
Score					
510 +					
490 – 509					
470 – 489					
450 – 469					
430 – 449					
410 – 429					
390 – 409					
370 – 389					
350 – 369					
330 – 349					
310 – 329					
290 – 309					
270 – 289					
250 – 269					
230 – 249					
210 – 229					
190 – 209					
170 – 189					
Round	1	2	3	4	5

Plot scores made on Flint Rounds on Table 8–6 to show progress being made.

Score					
TABLE 8-6					
Profile Record of Flint Round Scores					
155 +					
145 – 154					
135 – 144					
125 – 134					
115 – 124					
105 – 114					
95 – 104					
85 – 94					
75 – 84					
65 – 74					
55 – 64					
45 – 54					
35 – 44					
25 – 34					
15 – 24					
5 – 14					
0 – 4					
Round	1	2	3	4	5

ARCHERY SCORE CARD
Columbia Round

Name _____ Sec. _____

1							
2							
3							
4							

50-Yard Range Total

1							
2							
3							
4							

40-Yard Range Total

1							
2							
3							
4							

30-Yard Range Total

Columbia Round Total _____

FIELD ARCHERY SCORE CARD
FLINT ROUND

NAME _____ SEC. _____

1						1					
2						2					
3						3					
4						4					
5						5					
6						6					
7						7					

FIRST HALF _____ SECOND HALF _____

ROUND TOTAL _____

BIBLIOGRAPHY

Books

Ascham, Roger. *Toxophilus*. London: A. Murray & Son, 1545. 168 pp.

Written in the time of King Henry VIII, it is the first comprehensive treatise on the fundamentals of archery.

Boy Scouts of America. *Archery Merit Badge Series*. New York: Merit Badge Library, 1941. 77 pp., illus.

Merit badge requirements in archery. History, techniques of shooting, and tackle making for the beginner.

Burke, Edmund H. *Archery Handbook*. New York: Arco Publishing Co., 1954. 144 pp., illus.

The do-it-yourself series. The many illustrations show the techniques of shooting, the making of equipment, and hunting techniques.

Craft, Dave, and Cia Craft. *The Teaching of Archery*. New York: A. S. Barnes and Co., 1936. 82 pp., illus.

Duff, James. *Bows and Arrows*. New York: The Macmillan Company, 1927. 173 pp., illus.

A technical discussion of tackle making and shooting techniques by an experienced bowyer and archer.

Elmer, Robert P., and Nabih A. Faris. *Arab Archery*. Princeton, New Jersey: Princeton University Press, 1945. 182 pp., illus.

A translation of an Arabic manuscript of about A.D. 1500 on the excellence of the bow and arrow.

Elmer, Robert P. *Archery*. Philadelphia: The Penn Publishing Co., 1926. 456 pp.

History of world archery, development in America, and tackle making.

Elmer, Robert P. *Target Archery.* New York: Alfred A. Knopf Co., 1946. 154 pp., illus.

>History of archery in America, tackle making, and fundamentals are discussed.

————————. *The Book of the Long Bow.* New York: Doubleday, Doran and Co., 1929. 206 pp., illus.

>Readings about the English longbow.

Forbes, Thomas A. *Guide to Better Archery.* Harrisburg, Pa.: Stackpole Co., 1955. 307 pp., illus.

>Furnishes the desired know-how for every phase of archery from learning to shoot to hunting the elusive deer.

Ford, Horace. *Archery, Its Theory and Practice.* Toledo: F. E. Roff, 1880. 175 pp., illus.

>The fundamentals of archery thoroughly explained; point-of-aim theory.

Gordon, Paul H. *New Archery, Hobby, Sport, and Craft.* New York: Appleton-Century-Crofts, Inc., 1939. 423 pp., illus.

>A thorough treatise on archery. An answer to the question, "What makes archery attractive and popular?"

Hart, Dorothy Mae. "Factors Which Contribute to Success in Target Archery." Ph.D. thesis, State University of Iowa, 1955. Microcarded.

Hickman, C. N., F. Nagler, and Paul E. Kopsteg. *Archery: The Technical Side.* Redlands, California: Box 388 NFAA, 1947. 281 pp., illus.

>A detailed analysis of the physics of bows and arrows, compilation of scientific and technical articles.

Hill, Howard, *Hunting the Hard Way.* Chicago: Follett Publishing Co., 1953. 318 pp., illus.

>Fascinating accounts of game hunting of all kinds.

————————. *Wild Adventure.* Harrisburg, Pa.: Stackpole Co., 1954. 228 pp., illus.

>An absorbing collection of the true jungle thrills by an outstanding bow hunter.

Hochman, Louis. *The Complete Archery Book.* Greenwich, Conn.: Fawcett Publications, 1957. 144 pp., illus.

>The many illustrations help in explaining tackle making and the uses of archery.

Hodgkin, Adrian Eliot. *The Archer's Craft.* London: Faber & Faber, 1951. 222 pp., illus.

Explains making tackle, shooting, and hunting with bows.

Hoogerhyde, Russ, and Carl G. Thompson. *Archery Aims.* Pinehurst, N. C.: Archers Co., 1933. 54 pp., illus.

Common-sense shooting methods.

Hougham, Paul C. *The Encyclopedia of Archery.* New York: A. S. Barnes & Co., 1957. 202 pp., illus.

Hunt, W. Ben, and John J. Metz. *The Flat Bow.* New York: Bruce Publishing Co., 1948.

Good instructions for the amateur who wishes to make his own tackle.

Jaeger, Eloise. *How To Improve Your Archery.* Chicago: The Athletic Institute.

An abundant amount of illustrations with brief captions describing history, fundamentals, and rules—for the beginner.

Lambert, A. W. *Modern Archery.* New York: A. S. Barnes & Co., 1929. 306 pp., illus.

A textbook on the art of shooting.

Love, Albert J. *Field Archery Technique.* Corpus Christi, Texas: Dotson Printing Co., 1956. 121 pp., illus.

A comprehensive text that covers the subject of field archery.

National Field Archery Association. *Official Handbook of Field Archery.* Box H, Palm Springs, California.

A yearly publication covering rules, champions, and tournaments in field archery. Game statistics, shooting and hunting techniques also included.

Perry, Walter. *Bucks and Bows.* Harrisburg, Pa.: Stackpole Co., 1954. 223 pp., illus.

A good discussion of archery tackle, shooting techniques, and hunting deer.

Pope, Saxton. *Yahi Archery.* Berkeley: University of California Press, 1918.

The facts of archery of one tribe, the Yahi or Deer Creek Indians.

Pope, Saxton. *Hunting with Bow and Arrow* (new ed.). New York: G. P. Putnam's Sons, 1947. 257 pp., illus.

A classic on shooting and bow hunting. Dr. Pope learned archery from a full-blooded Indian named *Ishi.*

———————. *The Adventurous Bowmen.* New York: G. P. Putnam's Sons, 1926. 233 pp., illus.

Field notes on African archery in Tanganyika.

Reichart, Natalie, and Gilman Keasey. *Archery.* New York: A. S. Barnes & Co., 1940. 95 pp., illus.

The relaxed method of shooting is carefully outlined along with equipment, teaching methods, and types of competition. This book is better designed for teachers than for students.

Rhode, Robert J. *Archery Champions.* Norristown, Pa.: The Archer's Publishing Company, 1961. 212 pp., illus.

A record of champions and tournaments.

Rounsevelle, Phillip. *Archery Simplified.* New York: A. S. Barnes & Co., 1931. 120 pp., illus.

A description of the techniques of shooting, safety, and competition; mostly for instructors.

Stalker, Tracy L. *How To Make Modern Archery Tackle.* Casein Company of America, 350 Madison Avenue, New York 17, N. Y.: 1948. 34 pp.

Excellent instruction on how-to-do-it, for the home craftsman who desires to make his own tackle.

Sumpton, Dorothy. *Archery for Beginners.* Philadelphia: W. B. Saunders Co., 1932. 141 pp., illus.

A discussion of equipment, techniques, rules.

Thompson, Maurice, and Will Thompson. *How To Train in Archery.* New York: E. I. Horsman, 1879. 54 pp.

A complete study of the York Round.

Van Coevering, Jack, and Fred Bear. *Fun with Bow and Arrow.* Glencoe, Ill.: Free Press, 1953. 24 pp., illus.

A brief account of shooting techniques and tackle for the beginner.

Whiffen, Larry C. *Shooting the Bow.* Milwaukee: The Bruce Publishing Co., 1946. 83 pp., illus.

Describes the techniques of shooting.

Films

Available at Grayling Film Service, Grayling, Michigan: All 16 mm. sound and color.

African Safari
Arrow for a Grizzly
Art of Archery
Badland Bucks
Backcountry Bowhunt
Bow Fishing Fun
Bwana Bowmen
Kaibab Bucks
Prairie Pronghorn

Available at Albin Films, 85544 Sunset Blvd., Hollywood 46, California: 16-mm. movies of Howard Hill, Joe Fries, Ande Vail, Russ Hoogerhyde, and Jim Lynch. Free list available.

Available at the Athletic Institute, 209 S. State Street, Chicago 4, Illinois: *Archery Filmstrip*, 35 mm., on history, shooting, aiming, and rules.

Available at Mrs. E. B. Miller, 67 Old Stone Church Road, Upper Saddle River, New Jersey:

Dr. C. N. Hickman's Science Films:
The Archer's Paradox—Action of the arrow as it leaves the string, taken at 2000 frames per second.
The Release—Right-hand action on release and action of the arrow at 4000 frames per second.
Target Archery Technique—400 feet, color, 16-mm. film demonstration by Jean Lee, former National and World Champion. Technique analysis by Myrtle K. Miller, coach.

Periodicals

Archery—A Sportsman's Magazine Devoted to Hunting and Field. Official Publication of the National Field Archery Association, P.O. Box H., Palm Springs, California.

The Archer's Magazine. Published monthly by the Archer's Publishing Company, P.O. Box 832, Norristown, Pennsylvania. For bow hunters, field shooters, target shooters, and all sportsmen.